Journey of Remembrance

A Christmas in the Death Camps of Poland

Journey of Remembrance

A Christmas in the Death Camps of Poland

edited by
William M. Finnin, Jr., ThD

The Marshpiper Press
DALLAS

photo by Dion Mcinnis

In Memoriam

Gail Reese Ward
Nov 15, 1950 - Nov. 23, 2003

She modeled for us each day how to live joyfully
in the full presence of our own mortality.

(above right) Frieze at Warsaw Memorial.

contents

Memorial to the leaders of the Warsaw Ghetto Uprising, April 19 through May 16, 1943.

Foreword

Rick Halperin

Remembrance is a vital human activity. It shapes our links to the past and helps define us in the present. As human beings, we need clearly to remember the past to nurture our vision of a better future. In the West, the Holocaust plays a significant role in the memory and conscience of civilizations. The Nazis' premeditated attempt to obliterate peoples from the earth is today, some six decades afterwards, largely ignored and forgotten. Yet the evils of intolerance, racism, prejudice, and the horrors of ethnic cleansing that combined to produce the destruction of some 11 million people between 1933 and 1945 live on, and remain pervasive today.

The participants in our December 2002 journey visited sites where almost 3.5 million people perished. The Nazi goal was to eradicate them from the face of the earth and to then remove all traces of the instruments of their destruction: the camps were to be destroyed, the ground plowed over, and no traces or records of the slaughter were to be left. In essence, the goal was to leave no memory of these victims for future generations.

This journey was designed to pay tribute, in part, to those men, women and children who were destroyed in the camps at Treblinka, Sobibor, Belzec, Majdanek, Auschwitz and Birkenau. Before this journey, most participants said they had never even heard of Belzec, a place that during its ten-month operation in 1942 alone claimed the lives of nearly 600,000 people. As such, this trip was to reclaim the right of remembrance.

To be sure, the journey was also to honor those who survived the camp experience. It was, and remains, necessary to remember that the human spirit is capable of enduring and vanquishing the most unimaginable horrors that mankind can produce.

Time marches on, and soon no one, perpetrator or survivor, will be left to speak about the unspeakable. Many of the remaining structures have either already disintegrated or are in the process of decay. To visit the sites is to attempt to remember them as they were—places of horror, filth, death, screams and cries, moaning and agony. Today, of course, they are quiet, uncrowded, and solitary.

We have an obligation to remember what happened in those (and other) places, as well as the reasons why it happened and was allowed to happen, because we who are alive today have the responsibility at least to try to prevent it from happening again. The very fact that the dehumanization and destruction of "undesirables" continues in our own time should serve as a gruesome reminder that Nazi ideology is still alive and well and has been improved upon since 1945.

Our journey proved to be a concrete invitation to see our lives as inextricably linked to both the past and future, so that all peoples, individually or collectively, do not have to know of a world with genocide. One Belzec is enough.

In Hamburg, in April 1945, at the Bullenhuser Damm School, the Nazis hanged twenty young Jewish children and four adult males. The inscription there today in the memorial garden speaks precisely to the point of why we went to the camps:

WHEN YOU STAND HERE, BE SILENT;
WHEN YOU LEAVE HERE, BE NOT SILENT.

When Darkness Fell

Sherry Aikman

On December 18, 2002, a group of ten boarded an airplane bound for Poland. Our destinations were six death camps, some located in remote, rural areas with others just outside bustling metropolitan cities. We paid homage to the memory of those murdered at Treblinka, Sobibor, Belzec, Majdanek, Auschwitz 1, Birkenau, and the Warsaw Ghetto.

Those events that occurred in another time seem increasingly to belong to another world. Only a deliberate act of memory can reconnect them to a place in time...infuse them with a sense of their historical past.

Our trip was a pilgrimage. This recollection of feelings is my act of memory. These sites of human destruction were haunted by the phantoms of past events, no longer visible, only remembered. By themselves, these crumbling sites of destruction lack "the will to remember," for without a person's intention to remember, the ruins remain little more than inert pieces of the landscape.

As we begin our journey at DFW Airport.

Children in Auschwitz. A memorial pictorial exhibit.

A Journey of Remembrance and Reward

Erin O'Neil

It has been said, "The journey is the reward." My journey was a trip to Poland during Christmas 2002—my reward, immeasurable. On December 21, ten of us boarded a plane headed to Warsaw, Poland, where we began our ten-day exploration of the Nazi death camps to remember the victims of the Holocaust.

Those ten days took an imagined sense of history and gave it a reality. Prior to the trip, I had studied the Holocaust, Hitler, and the "Final Solution," but nothing I had read, watched, or heard could have completely prepared me for the stark, vast, and horrific truth that lay before me.

Each site contributed individually and distinctively to my collective experience. I hardly know where to begin to describe all that I saw and felt. Moreover, one very quickly runs out of adjectives to depict this expansive network of death. The camps were all designed with the same purpose—to kill. Oddly, however, they all convey an astonishing juxtaposition of beauty and ugliness, life and death.

One cannot deny the splendor of nature—the grounds covered in a glistening white blanket of snow, the trees pristine and majestic, the sun radiating light and warmth ever so exquisitely, all nestled in the peaceful solitude of the surrounding forests away from the bustling activity of everyday life.

Yet amidst the beauty lies devastation. These serene and lively images are contrasted, almost purposefully, with the ugliness of the barracks, the brutality of the guard towers and barbed wire, the wretchedness of the gas chambers and crematoriums, and the unfathomable mounds of material remains and actual human ash.

"Seeing is believing," and seeing first hand the methodically engineered, Nazi genocidal machine, I was overwhelmed by the reality of "man's inhumanity to man." These camps encompass such a tremendous sense of loss—dreams quashed, families destroyed, and lives cut short.

No matter the site, with each step I felt I was walking on hallowed ground. No matter the direction, death was in its path. At times I was overcome with emotions ranging from deep sadness to intense anger, all the while trying to grasp the seemingly simple questions of how and why.

But the sad truth is that there are no definite answers. There is only hope. As clichéd, simplistic, and perhaps even shocking as it may sound, hope is the resounding feeling that I walked away with. The memorials and remaining camps are left as a reminder to all who visit—a reminder of those lives lost and forever changed. It is as if their voices are crying out, screaming to us, "REMEMBER!" Remember the hope they had, and remember to carry it with us for all of our days and live the lives they were unable to.

From the Warsaw ghetto to our final destination of Birkenau, each site left an imprint on my memory that cannot be erased, for my eyes saw it, my heart felt it, and my mind will never forget it! I will remember and continue to hope!

Reflections

Warsaw

In the summer of 1942, Nazi occupation forces in Poland deported more than 300,000 of the 375,000 Jews of Warsaw to Treblinka, where they were executed. As the fate of their fellows became known, remaining Jews in Warsaw committed to resisting further efforts at annihilation. From April 19, 1943, through May 16, 1943, Jewish armed resistance inside the walled-off ghetto held against overwhelming Nazi attempts to deport the remaining Jews. According to the Holocaust Encyclopedia, the Warsaw Ghetto Uprising was the largest armed Jewish uprising and the first armed urban resistance in German-occupied Europe.

Like so many journeys, this one began before we set out. Al, Paul Kubiak, and I went to the Dallas Opera the night of the fourteenth to see *Hansel und Gretel*. During the intermission someone said, "I get uncomfortable when the subject of Germans and ovens comes up." I recalled how Pynchon evoked the same fairy-tale at the end of *Gravity's Rainbow*, as though the horrors of that time were childhood nightmares—terrible yet fascinating—coming true. "Children, the world is a terrible place, and not only that, but far worse than anything you can imagine." So we imagine the murderers speaking to their littlest victims, veiling yet revealing truth at the last moment, like the "Angel of Death"[1] in the camps.

There must have been, must be, a special pleasure in watching the destruction of innocence, in seeing the birth of a terrifying knowledge in the eyes of those little ones....*Hansel und Gretel* imposes such weight on innocence—isn't that what we mean when we call it *"heavily* didactic"? Mother knows best—and father, though a bit of a drunk, is cheerfully reassuring—and when the children go to sleep, fourteen angels watch do keep—and at the last moment, against all odds, the wicked witch obligingly steps into the oven herself, and all the children go free. How can we not be aware as we watch this happy ending that it has been staged for the benefit of the children in the audience, that, as Brecht reminds us at the end of *Die Dreigroschen Oper,* the king's riding messenger seldom shows up in time to stop the execution?

Humperdinck's opera premiered in the middle of the 1890s, a decade that saw in all the great cities of Europe and America a marked increase in reports of child abuse and child murder: in the London of Henry James, who wrote "The Turn of the Screw" and *The Other House* at this time; in the Vienna of Sigmund Freud, who founded his theory of the neuroses on the child's discovery of sexuality through witnessing what he called the "primal scene"—the child's parents making love—here misconceived as an act of terror. For the child, the "scene of instruction" is a scene of violence, bringing about the dawn of a knowledge too overwhelming for consciousness to bear. The child's discovery, we would say, is a misconstruction, an accident, but as an assault on the child's identity, it counts as a form of abuse.

All abuse is absurd, resting as it does on disproportion between means and end, between abuser and victim, and most of all that within the abuser's identity. The violence by means of which the abuser claims to be "disciplining" or "correcting" the victim bears no relation to whatever called it forth, nor is it part of a program of instruction, and since it is directed against victims who are weaker physically, we do it justice to call it a form of bullyism. The abuser walks in terror of having his own weakness revealed, and to prevent this revelation, he seeks victims who aren't likely to put up an effective fight.

The sick thing about the abusive personality is that it seeks to eliminate the absurdity at its core by identifying the inflicted bruises as tokens of love: a multiple misdirection in which rage and terror hide behind sorrow and love. And the terrible thing about this sickness is that it is contagious, and in no time at all the battered wife, the abused child, have also come to interpret their hurt, their pain, as signs of love. Love, they say, is a matter of will, and the will, notably headstrong, must be disciplined. "I must be cruel, only to be kind."

---

[1] Here I was thinking of Josef Mengele as portrayed by Robert Sean Leonard in the 1996 film *I Love You, I Love You Not*—another instance of the journey beginning before we set out, since this film was broadcast on cable shortly before we left for Warsaw. Darkly handsome in his S. S. uniform, Leonard smiles reassuringly as he leads twin girls to the site where he will experiment on them, leaving the twins' older sister to survive and remember and ultimately to pass the story of the Angel to her granddaughter. The scene plays out as macabre theater, as ritual even, and its stateliness projects an archaic myth onto our knowledge of Auschwitz and the other camps, for the Angel of Death is older by centuries than those obscene places and benign in many of his aspects. As Izra'il (Hebrew Azrael), he is numbered among the four archangels of Muslim tradition; when he writes our name in his book, we are born, and when he erases it, we die. In so doing, of course, he acts only as God wills. Forty days before the day appointed for our death, a leaf bearing our name falls from the tree that grows beneath the throne of God, and when Azrael sees it fall, he sets in motion our harvesting, consummated at the moment when our soul is threshed, so to speak, from our body.

John Lewis
December 23, 2002

Umschlagplatz staging area, for Jewish victims of the Warsaw Ghetto purge en route to Treblinka and other death camps.

Memorial to the leaders of the Warsaw Ghetto Uprising,
April 19 through May 16, 1943.

Warsaw

Umschlagplatz.

Reflections

Treblinka's anonymity as a tiny pastoral stop on an east Poland rail line was forever shattered when it became the final destination for almost 900,000 people from Europe and the shtetls across Poland. Razed by the Nazis in October of 1943, plowed under and replanted, then reconstructed as a rural farm, the camp today belies its grisly history...save for its 17,000 raw stone markers that shout to the present and future generations.

Treblinka today leaves an indelible impression with memorials that include the stunning sight of 17,000 jagged stones of various shapes and sizes on an open field representing the towns that lost Jews and others at the camp.

Ed Wisneski

Memorial obelisk to the almost 900,000 who died at Treblinka.

On this first morning, contrasts chill
    hoarfrost fixed to crystalline twig and branch
        untrod snow, crisp and layered,
            unspoiled purity belies the hidden horror

    endless silent woods stand sentry
        for unspeakable deaths
            here entombed
        and silent

17,000 stones in vigil stand
    weeping silent ice-tears for nine hundred thousand souls
        who will remember the one
           the forgotten many

On this cold morn, my heart clutches
    I choke
        I'll not forget.

William Finnin

Treblinka

Wooded walk.

Treblinka

Rail tie remains of train station at Treblinka.

Treblinka. Thousands of stones, placed in memory and honor of the victims of hatred. The plaque, in many languages, reads, "Never Again." I was moved the most by the little stones. To me, they represented the children. I wanted to touch one of the stones, but I didn't feel I was worthy. What have I got to offer that stone?

The contrast of the stones and the trees, glittering in the sunlight, was striking. The snow crunched under our boots. Without saying a word, we made a lot of noise. It was like wearing clumsy shoes and clomping through a church, each step breaking the silence that should be respected and observed.

Gail Ward
December 23, 2002

Remembrances at Treblinka

Treblinka, a place where nearly 900,000 human beings died, and there is little evidence of the camps, only a forest, fields, and burial pits.

The juxtaposition of the camp's current tranquil beauty with its horrendous history unsettles. This is an organic memorial of simple, lasting materials from the earth, a place where human souls and nature rest harmoniously. A giant obelisk-type boulder, weather-worn and sheer-sided, marks an open field packed by innumerable smaller stones of various shapes and size—none taller than five feet, some as small as telephone books. Except for successful efforts at remaining erect, each stone is unique.

Bordering the field railroad tracks, the coffin-like slabs of concrete only hint at the horror hidden here. Large upright stones, all similarly jagged in size and cut, stand sentinel. From the right angle, they seem to layer themselves deeply and evenly towards the horizon. Covered in snow, they stand as guardians of this space and bear a message. "No more death will ever be brought to this place." Treblinka has been reclaimed by nature.

And nature truly decorates Treblinka in grace and glory this day. The sun shines on unbroken snow blanketed seven to eight inches deep. The snow rests gently on the top of each stone in the memorial as well, dressing it in prismatic light. Hoar frost enhances the air above the denser snow, adding dimension to what was formerly invisible space. In the evergreens surrounding the field the hoar frost settles lightly on top of individual pine needles. With the slightest breath the ice crystals drop from the branches like practically weightless air. If the breath is more than slight, the crystals explode in a burst of confetti-like light before winding slowly to the ground.

When I think about the atrocities at Treblinka and then consider what I viewed this day in December about 60 years later, all I can suggest to reconcile the contrasting realities is that Nature has retrieved what humans obliterated years ago. The tranquility I witnessed is Nature's attempt at healing our past atrocities...laying a salve on humanity's wounds.

kathleen edwards

Reflections

Sobibor

Isolated in the forests outside Warsaw, Sobibor's tree-filled landscape belies the horror of its history. The killing at Sobibor began in April 1942. Before operations ended nineteen months later, more than 250,000 Jews died within its boundaries, murdered by their Nazi wardens. Sobibor was the scene of a prisoner uprising in 1943 that precipitated the executions of more than 40,000 prisoners across the Reich in retribution.

I watched as Rick made a solemn, solitary journey around the huge mound, gently brushing the snow off the very edge with his hand, obviously in physical and spiritual communion with all who rested there.

I watched as Will emerged from the back side of the mound, heard him singing ever so softly. He stopped before the mound and removed his hat, despite the freezing cold. Such a simple, pure gesture of respect. I started to cry. I rejoined Lin a few yards from the mound, clung to him, crying softly. As always, he comforted me.

It was very quiet, with the snow blanketing all sound. Even our footsteps were muted, much more so than at Treblinka. I thought of the guard tower near the entrance and the mound at the end of the road. I felt I should shake my fist and curse the tower and kneel in prayer at the mound. I did neither.

Gail Ward

Sobibor

Secreted deep in the forest, unexpectedly, a guard tower remained. Menacing. Eerie. Down a road, lined with trees, stood a statue made of red stone—a face filled with agony. At the end of the road, a cement-encased mound, perfectly symmetrical covered in snow—a mound of human ashes. Tears rolled down my face.

Gail Ward

Monument to the murdered victims at the Sobidor death camp, active between 1942 and 1943.

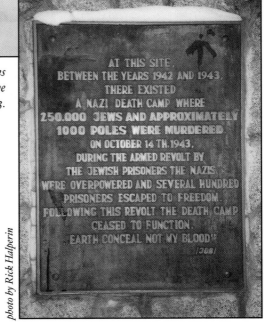

AT THIS SITE
BETWEEN THE YEARS 1942 AND 1943,
THERE EXISTED
A NAZI DEATH CAMP WHERE
250,000 JEWS AND APPROXIMATELY
1000 POLES WERE MURDERED.
ON OCTOBER 14 TH. 1943,
DURING THE ARMED REVOLT BY
THE JEWISH PRISONERS THE NAZIS
WERE OVERPOWERED AND SEVERAL HUNDRED
PRISONERS ESCAPED TO FREEDOM
FOLLOWING THIS REVOLT THE DEATH CAMP
CEASED TO FUNCTION.
"EARTH CONCEAL NOT MY BLOOD"
/3081

Reflections
Majdanek

Built as an extermination and labor camp, Majdanek began its killing operations in April 1942 and ended in July 1944. Majdanek represents the unholy alliance between Nazi genocidal policies and German business practice. Operated in conjunction with the Daimler industrial conglomerate as one of their munitions installations, Majdanek provided ample labor for the war-machine while feeding the furnaces of Hitler's Final Solution.

Just outside Lublin is Majdanek. A mammoth stone monument marks the entrance. It's hard to describe. It could be letters, forming a word in Polish. Or it could be simply an abstract representation of sentiments. Regardless of any symbolism, it does stand as a sentry, guarding the extensive grounds of the camp.

A two-story, white building stands outside the fences. The camp commandant's home. All I could think of was "pure, unadulterated evil resided there." I wondered if allowed to enter the house, I could still sense the evil. Did it permeate the walls? Contaminate the dwelling forever?

An intact gas chamber exists at Majdanek. As we entered in single file, someone said, "I'm not sure I want to go in." How many thousands of people voiced that same sentiment, all those years ago! There they were, the showerheads—just like you'd read and heard about—and yet I still thought, "My God, they actually existed!"

Standing on the very spot where thousands of people had once stood facing execution, my faith in a loving God was shaken to its very core. I stood there, openly crying, and silently asked the question, "When people cried out to God for help, what was the response to their cries? Was there a response? Or only deafening silence?" I was crying and so very, very angry.

Only one of the buildings that displayed victims' belongings was open—the one that contained their shoes, thousands and thousands of shoes in wire bins. Why did I expect they would all be prison-issue shoes, all alike except for size? There were work boots and street shoes and sandals and party shoes. One pair in particular caught my eye—a beautifully styled, chic pair of high heels. They prompted a flood of questions to rush into my mind. "Who was she, the woman who wore those shoes? What must she have looked like, walking into Majdanek in those elegant shoes? And why was she wearing them that day? Did she know where she was going when she dressed that morning?" Perhaps not profound questions, but they forced me to picture a woman living a normal life, suddenly and brutally interrupted, and then ended.

I consciously took multiple deep breaths before climbing the last two steps. Church bells began to ring in the distance, their timing exquisite yet eerie. It was Christmas day.

Thousands and thousands of victims' shoes piled into wire bins.

I walked up the steps to the mausoleum alone. Under a massive domed roof made of stone lay the enormous mound of human ashes. It was unimaginable and indescribable.

As I walked down the steps, I talked to the victims, silently, inside my head. I told them they had not been forgotten—that the living still cry for them, pray for them, mourn their loss. I hoped they found some comfort in that because for whom among us will the same be true, when we are gone. And then I chastised myself, realizing/remembering that where their souls now reside, they have no need to be comforted by us...by me.

Driving away, I looked over at the memorial. Children were sledding down its side. That was wrong! That was so very wrong!

Gail Ward
December 25, 2002

A great dome covers the mausoleum of exposed ashes, and to its right a squat building with tall chimney: the crematorium and gas chamber complex.

Majdanek still looks as though the Nazis left in a hurry the night before. The place made my blood run cold. All the macabre tools they used to kill and burn their victims are still there, remarkably undamaged by time—the "showerheads" in the gas chambers, the ovens in the crematorium, the truck chassis on which they burned Jews before the crematorium was built, the table used to extract gold and silver from the teeth of corpses, the guard towers, the double rows of electrical wire fences, even unused canisters of Zyklon B gas the Nazi guards dropped through holes in the ceilings of the gas chambers. In the far distance from the entrance to the camp, beyond the remaining barracks, a domed structure rising from the ground like a bubble loomed ominously on the horizon. Up close, it was a chilling sight—a mausoleum covering the ashes of the dead—350,000 victims in a pile of dust.

Ed Wisneski

Human ashes beneath the mausoleum dome.

Approaching the monument, a huge stone monolith, you are dwarfed in body and mind by its size. Symbolically, the remains of a wrought iron gate, unconnected to anything and padlocked with a chain, stands at the head of the monument. Walking toward it, you must descend into a symbolic valley of death. Sharp stones protrude on both sides, covered this day with soft snow. We climbed out of the valley to the base of the monument and stood transfixed by the view. Looking down an arrow-straight road, one mile long, open fields on the left, barracks on the right, we could see in the distance, at the very end of the road, a great dome covering the mausoleum of exposed ashes, and to its right a squat building with tall chimney: the crematorium and gas chamber complex. It takes nearly twenty minutes to walk this path. The frozen ground numbed my feet. The view before me numbed my soul.

"Let our fate be your warning" is the inscription on the stone in front of the mausoleum.

Sherry Aikman

The Waffen-SS used Zyklon-B poison gas to end the lives of more than 360,000 persons at Majdanek and sold more than 4,000 bales of human hair to companies employed by the Reich in making military clothing.

From the "shower" rooms to the ovens. The ovens at Majdanek were fed thousands.

The gas chambers, with showerheads that rained gas.

The ovens.

On this cold Christmas morning, I walk alone where untold others met their deaths in fiery pits and crowded showers, from gallows hung, on jagged wires now rusted in new snow, by poison gas and gagging, bullets quick but lethal nonetheless. I seek to fathom twisted human spirits whose hate makes these rough stone monuments eternally necessary. I am overwhelmed with the order and the horror of this place.

I imagine entering a shower on such a morning as this, stripped bare, shivering under cold trickles. Icy spikes pierce my skin. Packed so tight against these strangers I lose my breath. Then smell the gas, choke, fight constrictions of larynx, gasp unable to move, know my end is near, feel only the press of others in death-throe's horror, then leave this earth forever simply because...because I am a Jew.

William Finnin

Majdanek....Could it be colder? Bleaker? Frozen mists hug ice-clad roads as we lumber from the bus and sense the immensity of this factory of death. Here we are, erstwhile pilgrims in this frozen land, seeking some resolution to decades-old questions: "How could this horror have come to pass?"

The beauty of mist and morning do not support the terror that shaped this place, deflect the images that marked the moments of those who came here to die. In the distance...towers, church spires...each reminds that Majdanek was no isolated island.

William Finnin

Reflections

Belzec

Belzec, near the Poland-Ukraine border, was the most isolated camp we visited. In December 2002, a single marker, six feet square by two high, signified the only memorial. Snow covered trails, apparent ash-laden burial mounds, and an expanse of woods belied the deaths of over 600,000 persons, mostly Jews, in this hilly forest. Today a newly constructed memorial and museum honors those who perished and preserves their memory.

At Belzec, there is virtually nothing to identify its notorious past except a nondescript block of rock citing the number of victims and the dilapidated train station where Jews were unloaded from crammed freight cars, stripped, and marched to the gas chambers. The United States Holocaust Memorial Museum and the Polish government have raised money to build a monument and museum in the future.

Ed Wisneski

Trees planted to cover razed barracks.

Memorial monolith.

Auschwitz is the legend, the one we all grew up with—the one that you automatically think of when you reflect on Nazi death camps. Belzec we never heard of. At Belzec, more than 600,000 died. On the day we visited, there was no trace of the horror that took place there. It was as if the entire town was in denial.

William Finnin

Offloading platform at Belzec.

Reflections
Auschwitz

Auschwitz 1, "Stammlager," outside Krakow, served as a Polish military base before its appropriation by Nazis as a prison and death camp, primarily for political prisoners. Today its barracks, gallows, killing wall, gas chamber, and crematorium stand as gruesome reminders of the horrific ends more than 40,000 prisoners came to there.

Museum gallery in Auschwitz barracks.

Photos from documents and records of Auschwitz prisoners.

Charcoal drawings of the execution wall.

Victims' prosthetics.

Personal eating utensils, plates and cups.

Execution wall.

Arbeit Macht Frei ("Work Makes One Free") spans the gateway.

Reflections

Birkenau

photo by Rick Halperin

Birkenau's seemingly endless rows of barracks and guard towers, rail lines, seven gas chambers, and open-air crematoria make plain the systematic premeditation of Hitler's "Final Solution." For those who entered Birkenau by rail, death on work crews or in gas chambers was almost certain. It is estimated that up to 2.5 million persons were killed in the three Auschwitz complexes, most of them eastern European Jews.

Main gate, Birkenau.

*Railway inside Birkenau leading
directly to the gas chambers.*

Guard tower.

Birkenau

Crematorium ventilation grids.

Birkenau barracks.

Our memorial candles, one of many memorial plaques.

Forever let this place be a cry of despair and a warning to humanity, where the Nazis murdered about one and a half million men, women, and children, mainly Jews, from various countries of Europe.

Auschwitz - Birkenau 1940-1945
(plaque above)

To See or Not to See, That is the Question

Ed Wisneski

I s it constructive to preserve sites where killing and suffering took place, no matter how gruesome the evidence might be? Is it better to bury all the grim reminders that haunt the grieving relatives of the victims, or is it disrespectful to eradicate anything they feel memorializes their lost ones?

"The Murder of Emmett Till"—a documentary that recently aired on PBS—showed Mamie Till Mobley's courageous response to these types of questions. Her 14-year-old son Emmett was brutally killed in Money, Mississippi, in the summer of 1955 because he accepted a dare from a friend and allegedly called a white woman "baby" and whistled at her.

Instead of hiding the butchered remains of her son—he had one ear torn off, an eye gouged out, and a bullet hole in his head—Mobley encouraged *Jet* magazine to publish the gut-wrenching photo of Emmett for all to see. She insisted on an open-casket funeral and held off the burial for four days so all who came to pay their respects could see.

"I wanted the world to see what I had seen," said Mobley, who died on January 6 at the age of 81.

During the week of Christmas, my wife and I accompanied Southern Methodist University human rights instructor Rick Halperin and seven others to see the remains of what Jews had seen in Poland during World War II.

The Nazis' ethnic cleansing began just 14 years before Emmett Till's body was fished out of the Tallahatchie River with a 70-pound cotton-gin fan around his neck. Unlike concentration camps such as Dachau, the Polish death camps existed solely to provide the means to complete Hitler's "Final Solution" of wiping Jews off the face of the earth. With sickening, sociopathic precision, the Nazis' three-year blitzkrieg of murder in Poland killed almost as many Jews as three times the entire population of the Dallas-Forth Metroplex.

Our group trudged alone in single-digit temperatures on the hallowed grounds of the windy, desolate, snow-covered camps of mass murder in Eastern Poland—Treblinka, Sobibor, Majdanek, and Belzec—as well as the more-visited Auschwitz and Birkenau camps.

Halperin made a wise choice to expose us to the four remote camps in the dead of winter where the solitude and serenity magnified the impact immensely. He constantly took photos to use in his class. I asked how his students reacted when he discussed the Polish death camps. He said that 90 percent of them wanted to know why they had never heard of these places.

That's why it's important to keep the "coffin lids" open.

If we do not preserve sites of infamy, if we do not build monuments and museums to show what happened and to honor both the survivors and the deceased, we commit a disservice to those who do not know the truth as well as to those who do. If we allow all the physical remains of horror to deteriorate into nothing and fail to provide some sort of remembrance, we dishonor those who perished and perpetuate the anonymity and deception the perpetrators sought to maintain.

In Poland, the Nazis tried to eliminate all traces of their murders. They succeeded at Treblinka, where 900,000 people were annihilated, and Belzec, where 600,000 were obliterated in only nine months. The Nazis actually built farmhouses, ploughed the land, and planted trees and crops to disguise those areas.

As we drove away from Majdanek, we saw children sliding on sleds down the hill where a huge monument is located. The scene made me think of the 1.5 million Jewish youths snuffed out by the Nazis. I hoped that those children knew why the memorial was there. I am grateful to those responsible for leaving everything as it was at Majdanek and maintaining it for 60 years. They even keep it open on December 25. I had never heard of the place. Now I will never forget it.

That's why it's important to keep the "coffin lids" open.

The Pilgrims

The common thread of SMU brought us together, but the common experiences of Polish winter, Nazi death camps, endless miles together across Polish countryside, and shared meals held us together and fashioned our group into that small but vibrant pilgrimage community we became.

sherry aikman

Sherry Aikman, photographic chronicler for our pilgrimage to Poland, has served as administrative assistant for The Women's Center at Southern Methodist University. A graphic artist, she has recently relocated to Fredericksburg, Texas, where she helped found and manages a creative design stationery store.

kathleen edwards

Currently serving as a residence hall director at Xavier University in Cincinnati, Ohio, kathleen has served as an AmeriCorps* VISTA at a homeless shelter in Dayton. kathleen lives her days working with students and advocates for men, women, and families experiencing homelessness. She's a practicing vegan and chronic nomad, who eventually hopes to thru-hike the Appalachian Trail.

william finnin

William M. Finnin, Jr., ThD, is Chaplain and Minister to the University at Southern Methodist University and has served on the Board of Directors of the Dallas Center for Holocaust Studies and chair of the Jewish-Christian Relations Committee of the Greater Dallas Community of Churches. He has presided over an inter-faith service of memory on the occasion of Yom HaShoah annually since 1983.

rick halperin

Rick Halperin, PhD, is a lifelong human rights activist. He has been teaching Human Rights in the History Department at Southern Methodist University since 1985. Rick was Chair of the Board of Directors of Amnesty International USA in 1992 and is the current President of the Texas Coalition to Abolish the Death Penalty.

john lewis

After receiving his undergraduate and graduate degrees from Harvard, John Lewis joined the SMU English Department in 1970. He has remained there ever since, where his teaching duties include American literature, medieval studies, and linguistics. For over twenty years he wrote reviews and articles, mainly on film and theater, for the *Dallas Observer* and the *Met*, local alternative newsweeklies.

erin o'neil

Erin O'Neil received her BA in Radio, Television, and Film from the University of North Texas and her MLA from SMU in May 2003. Currently she is Manager of Academic Ceremonies and Office Operations in the Office of the Provost at SMU. She has studied with Dr. Rick Halperin at SMU.

gail and linton ward

Gail Ward has spent the majority of her career in higher education, directing programs that serve students, faculty, staff, and members of the community. Most recently, she has served as the coordinator of the Women's Symposium at Southern Methodist University.

Linton Ward worked as a civil engineer for several years. After volunteering as the construction liaison in the building of a new church, he earned a second degree in computer science and now works as a programmer analyst for Southwest Airlines.

Married for 23 years and counting, they have traveled down many paths together, celebrating the joys and facing the challenges they have encountered along the way. They journeyed to Poland to pay tribute and bear witness at sites of unspeakable horror. They returned inspired by the courage, faith and hope demonstrated by the victims and survivors of the Holocaust; with a heightened appreciation for the precious gift of their marriage; and with a renewed commitment to the pursuit of peace throughout the world.

ed & susan wisneski

Ed Wisneski, MA, MLA, MTh, is Senior Associate Athletic Director at Southern Methodist University and chaplain assistant in the Office of the Chaplain there. His travelogue writing has chronicled his global travels in major newspapers across the nation.

Susan Wisneski, MA, is a substance-abuse counselor in Dallas, where she specializes in multiple-diagnosis treatment and support of persons who are HIV positive.

Holocaust Remembered

Linton Ward

The atrocities that occurred in Poland and surrounding countries in the 1930s and 1940s are now even harder for me to comprehend after having walked along the same paths where millions took their final steps. These countless ones went, some willingly, with the hope of a new and brighter future, only to find suffering, hopelessness, and death waiting for them under the heavy hand of Nazi SS officers. Millions went, only to be shot to death as their countrymen watched, only to be herded into concrete-walled rooms with family, friends, and strangers, slowly to die by suffocation from poisonous gas. How could it go on so long, day after day, year after year? How could one human do that to another human? I still have a hard time comprehending the duration and scope of the killing that took place. Death did not pause for time of day or for change in season. While the faces changed at the camps and the camps themselves changed throughout the course of the war, only death itself remained constant.

Sixty years after the war, it is impossible to imagine what the camps were really like. At Auschwitz, the layout of the buildings, trees, and roads gave me the sense that I was on a college or corporate campus. Indeed, I was on a campus,...but not a campus where students studied or business associates conducted business. This camp was designed and built for one purpose only—the elimination of a people.

We journeyed during the Christmas season, and because of the holiday, few visitors were present. Auschwitz was very quiet the day we arrived. The sun was out, but the ground was covered in snow and the air was very cold, so cold that my exposed nose and ears quickly felt the sting of that winter day. The quiet and harshness of the cold sharpened senses; I absorbed my surroundings. The discomfort I felt from the cold paled in comparison to what the prisoners must have endured. With little clothing and food, just surviving the elements would have been a formidable task in itself, not to speak of the punishment and torture handed out by the Nazis.

While the buildings, sidewalks, and roads identify the physical camp, Auschwitz-Birkenau is today constructed with the sights, sounds, and smell of death. Images of death, dying, pain, suffering, fear, anguish, crying, screaming, and prayer today fill the air throughout the camp.

59

Barking guard dogs, machine gun and pistol fire, Nazi officers screaming orders, and the sound of lash and whip on flesh define this death camp in memory and in mind. Smells of burning flesh and bone from the crematory were surely the most wretched component of the camp, a sweet scent, such as the smell of bread baking. But once one learned the source of that scent, how could there be any hope of surviving? Could there be any hope at all?

It now made sense that the Nazis built Auschwitz, as well as the other camps, far away from cities out in the wilderness. They had to hide their actions from the rest of humanity in order to carry out their mission of death. The absence of those sights, sounds, and smells today makes it impossible to experience the camps as they really were. I have only my imagination for that.

As we visited other camps throughout Poland, I noticed something inside me gradually building and quite foreign: hatred—hatred of the Nazis, hatred of the German people, hatred of the human race. I realized, however, that it was precisely that kind of hatred that fueled Nazi Germany's rain of death and destruction on the Jews, on Poland, and on Europe. After reflection on my beliefs and faith, my only solution to cope with such hatred was to rid myself of it by turning it over to God. I do not think that any reasonable person could take on the horrors of the Holocaust and not feel some hatred. But once recognized, that hatred must be released, and God is there to take it from you.

I will always remember the December 2002 visit to Poland. The cold weather, the wonderful Polish food, the friendly people, and, of course, the camps. I was overwhelmed by what I witnessed at the camps and what I learned about the Holocaust, so overwhelmed that I feel the need for resolve somehow. It is my hope that someway all evil perpetrated by mankind, throughout all time, can be forgiven by God and forgotten by all of mankind and that all of humanity can exist as one, in Love, with God for eternity.

At the End

Sherry Aikman

Emotions too difficult to describe at the moment of experience now come flooding into my consciousness. The beauty of the sunset outside my home transports me back to the woods of Treblinka, Belzec, and Sobibor. I close my eyes and shiver, remembering the cold rising from the snow covered ground. I hear the crunch of our boots as we walked those sacred grounds...grounds now covered in pure white, keeping from our sight those remaining fragments of ash and bone that are still part of the landscape.

We were the only visitors at these sites, making it all the more surreal. Ours were the only footprints. Ours were the only tears. Each time, as we boarded the bus to journey on, our collective silence screamed our collective pain. At Belzec, we searched frantically for some physical remembrance of the lives that were taken there. We did not know at the time that all the monuments that had been there had been removed in preparation for a future museum and memorial. We walked through the woods. We crossed the railroad tracks. We looked for their peace and found it in the setting sun as we made our way back to the bus.

Rick spoke of our experience transforming future Christmas gatherings. But in reality, it has gone beyond a time or place. I am transformed by a cloud, a sunset, an emotion. Tears well up when the vision of Majdanek's mausoleum flashes in my mind's eye. So many lost, so many dreams unfulfilled. The coldness of our Christmas day created a haze that hung over the site. It brought numbness to the body and numbness to the soul.

How could this have happened? Why did no one stand in their defense? Today, while the same processes are in action around the world, why do we not stand in defense of human rights? Why do we not hear their voices whispering in the wind, "Let our fate be your warning"?

Benediction

William Finnin

At the close of our afternoon at Birkenau we stood together, then-weary pilgrims gathering our souls and thoughts around the Memorial Plaque, lighting candles of remembrance. In the frigid stillness of those moments, punctuated by the near-imperceptible movements of three deer at the border woods beyond the gas chambers, it became quite clear that the days we had spent together and the places we had journeyed had changed us.

Your words, shared in this small volume, chronicle some of those changes. Your words bear witness to profound experiences shared during those wintry days in December 2002 at the edges of history's rationality. Your words, your insights, and observations hallow the memory of those who perished in one of history's darkest hours.

Perhaps the most poignant moment of our journey for me took place as we departed Belzec, that isolated setting bereft of markers, scrubbed clean of the horrors those woods had hidden. Our walks through those pristine, snow-covered woods put the lie to the well-constructed Nazi cover-up, the carefully architected falsehood, that death had not visited those wooded hills. We became, in those moments, witnesses forever against the failure of memory. That, in its largest context, had been the purpose of our journeying, and at Belzec—as at Treblinka and Sobibor, Majdanek, Auschwitz I and Birkenau—we remembered. We remember still.

Acknowledgements

When Dr. Rick Halperin became assistant director of the Office of Community Outreach and Volunteer Service, one of his first visits was to the Office of the Chaplain, where he proposed to me a campus wide pilgrimage to the Death Camps of Poland, to be undertaken in the dead of winter over Christmas Day 2002. Rick and I issued the invitation that fall, and eight members of the SMU community responded, constituting our pilgrimage contingent.

Lewis Gibbons at Mustang Travel put together an economical travel package, and a generous gift from SMU Trustee Sherrill Pettus made possible first class ground transport across frozen Poland. Sherry Aikman served as our official photographer and chronicler, presenting each traveler with a leather-bound journal in which to record reflections *en route* and creating a digital record of the group's photographic efforts. Without Sherry's photographic vision, this book would not have come together.

The idea of this volume was born in conversation with True Faust, graphic designer and editor of scores of books and magazines across 30 years of devotional and professional service. The Marshpiper Press is our creation, and this book bears its logo imprint. Early in the project, Dr. Albert H. Halff and Linton Ward generously provided funds to underwrite a portion of the production and printing costs.

Any errors found in this volume, of either typography or editorial judgment, are solely mine. The insights and creative moments here recorded belong to the collective experience and talent of our pilgrimage group. It has been a personal privilege to read and work with your creative insights and gifts. My hope has been to be true to your intentions if not always to your precise words, only because of limitations of space. The true gift, however, received in abundance throughout our journeys in Poland is the privilege of remembrance coupled with the obligation of witness to the atrocities committed in those six Nazi death camps.

We shall never forget.

William Finnin